BOOK 1

W9-BQE-731

Grand Trios for Piano

4 EARLY ELEMENTARY PIECES FOR ONE PIANO, SIX HANDS

Melody Bober

Trio playing is both energizing and exciting, and there are many ensemble possibilities: a teacher and two students; a parent and two siblings; or, my favorite, three friends. While performances can be thrilling, preparing trio music can be enjoyable as well since sharing the love of music with others is so rewarding.

Trios also offer a great musical experience for students. Rhythm, phrasing, articulation, and dynamics all become wonderful teaching tools while students learn to listen for that unique blending of parts. I have written *Grand Trios for Piano*, Book 1, so that today's piano students can experience music in a variety of styles, meters, and tempos. I have also written this collection so that students can progress technically and musically...together!

I sincerely hope that students will find the pieces challenging and fun in these *Grand Trios for Piano*!

Best wishes,

Melody Bober

CONTENTS

Alfred

Alfred Music Publishing Co., Inc.
P.O. Box 10003
Van Nuys, CA 91410-0003
alfred.com

ISBN-10: 0-7390-7932-8
ISBN-13: 978-0-7390-7932-4

Cover Photos
stage lights: © stock.xchng/photos71

Clapping Tune

Melody Bober

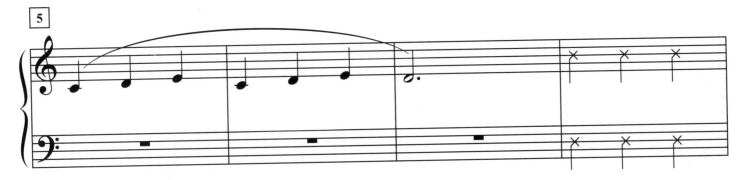

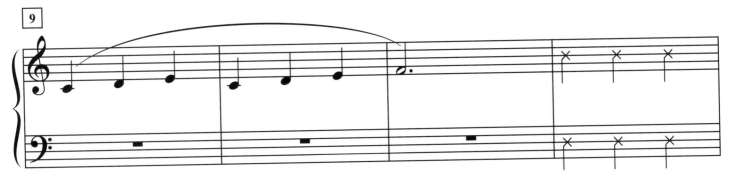

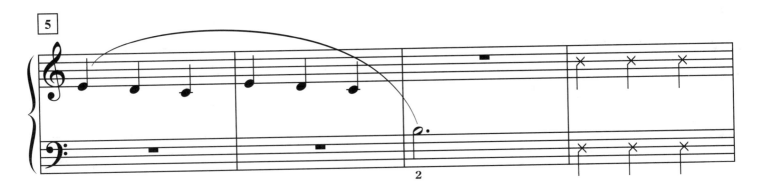

4

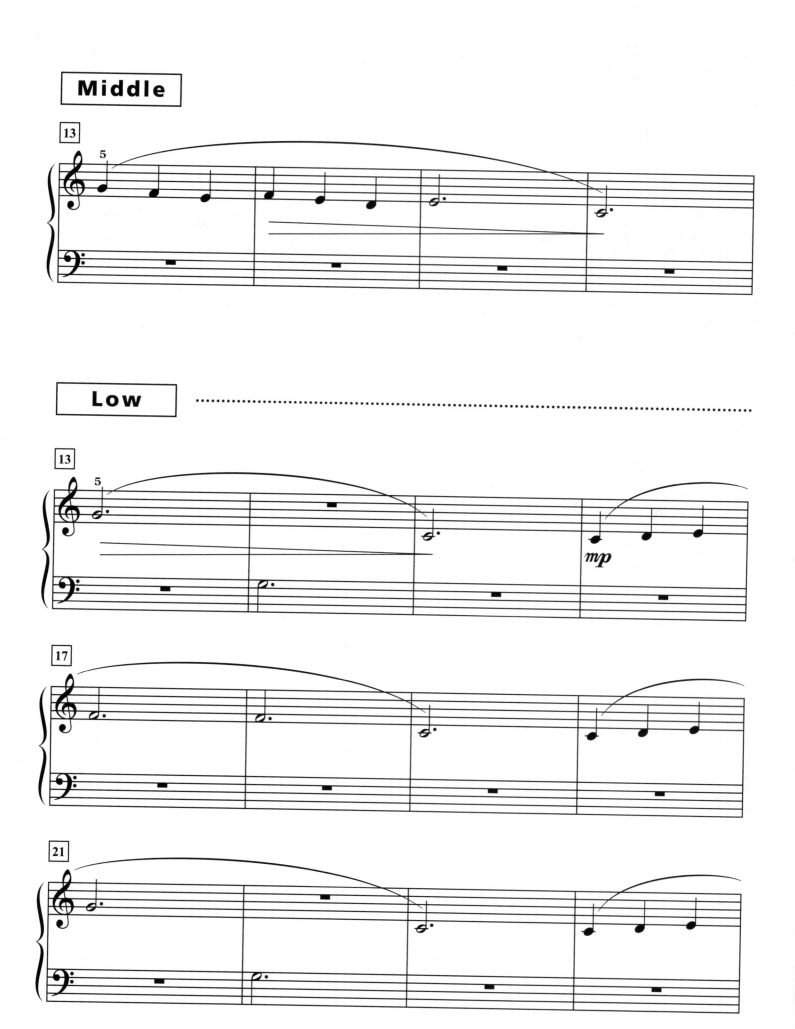

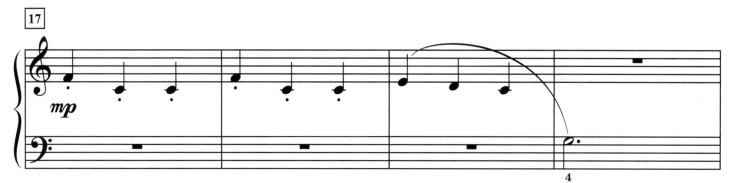

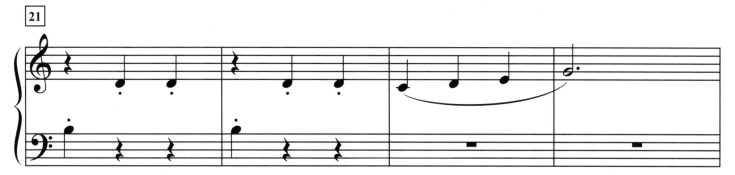

High

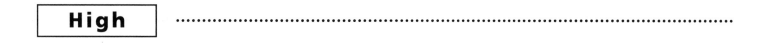

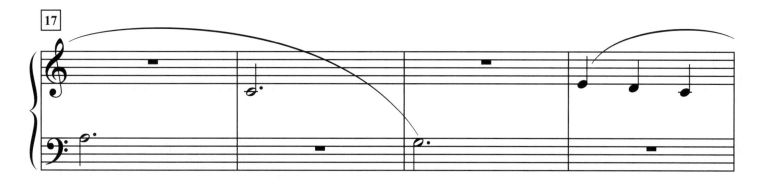

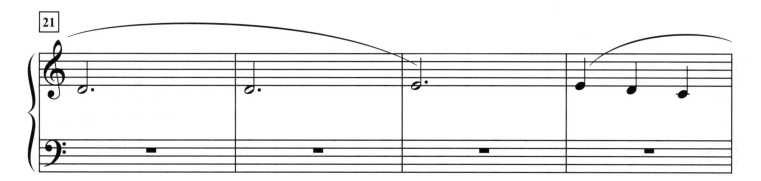

Middle

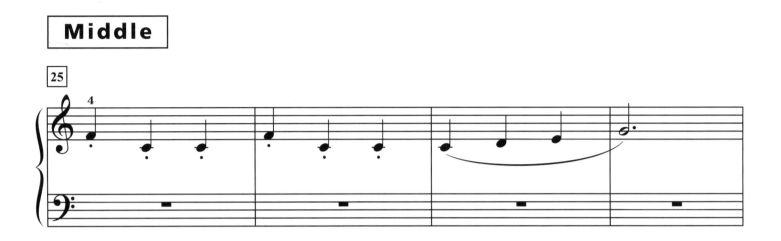

Low

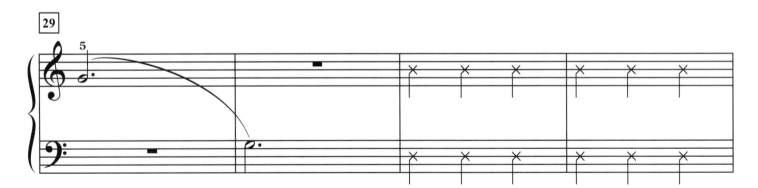

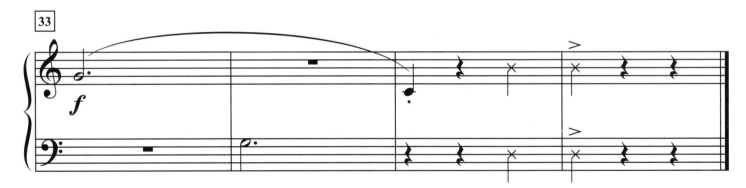

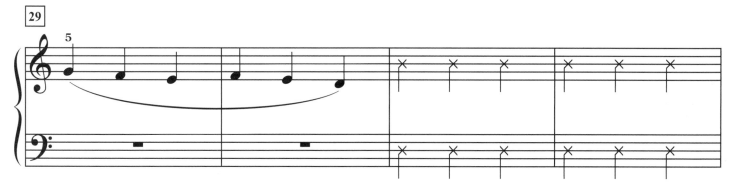

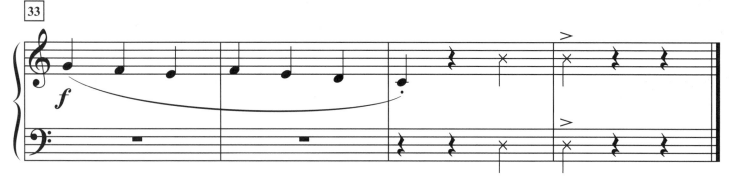

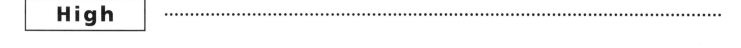

High

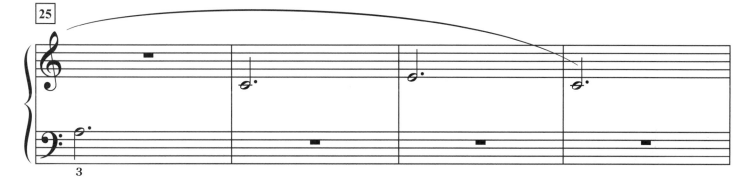

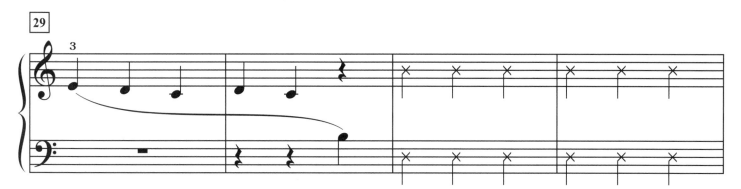

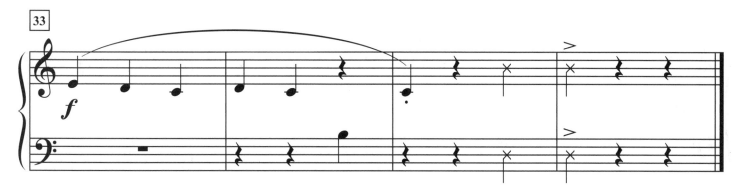

Owls at Midnight

Melody Bober

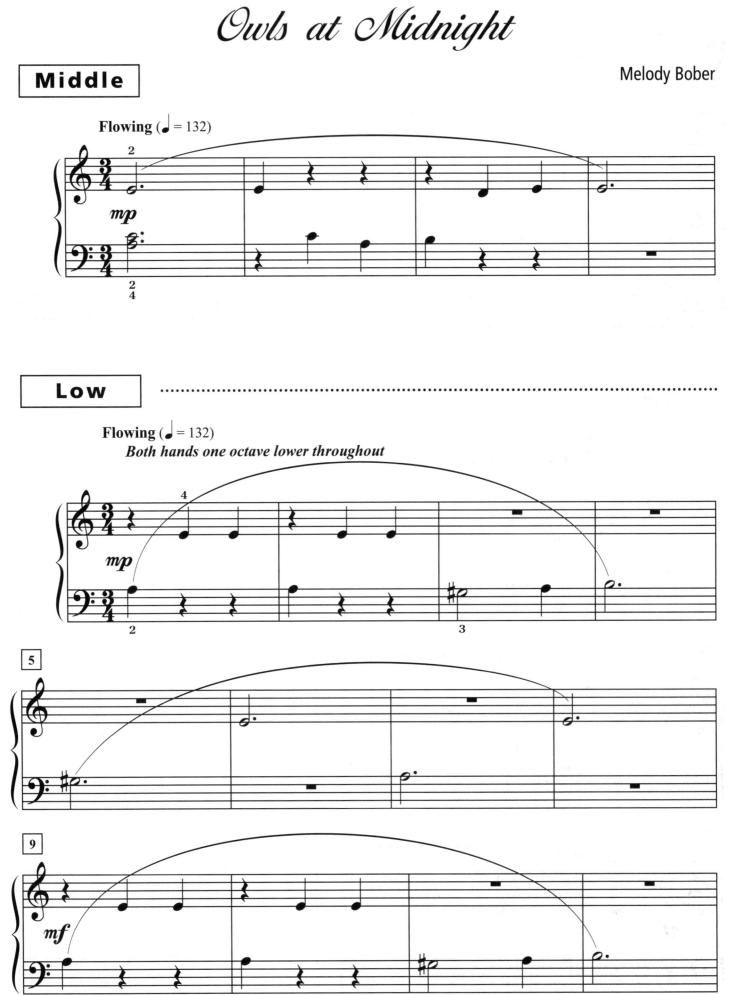

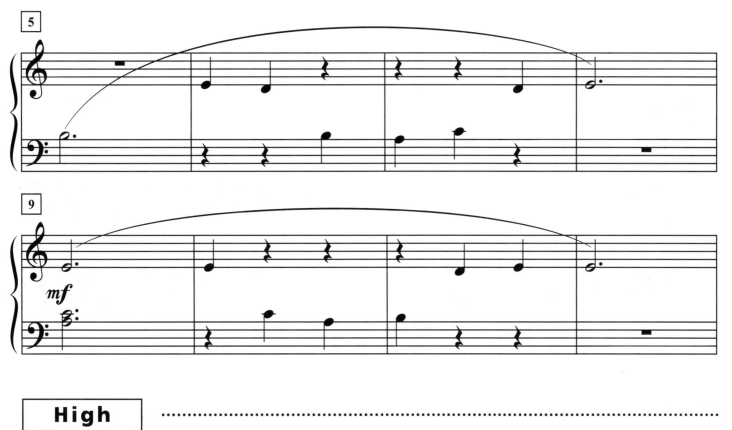

High

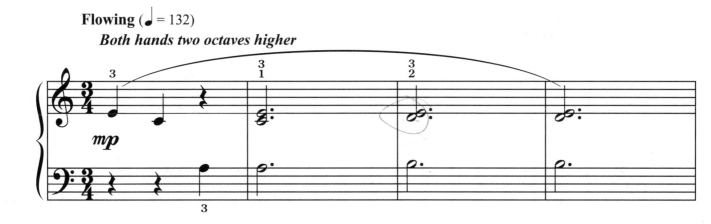

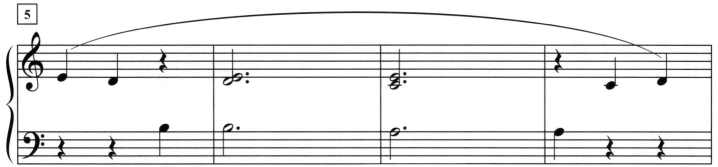

Middle

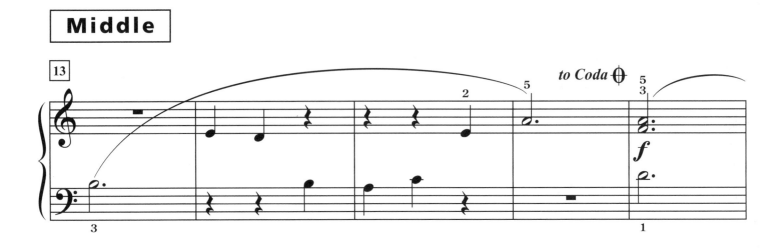

Low

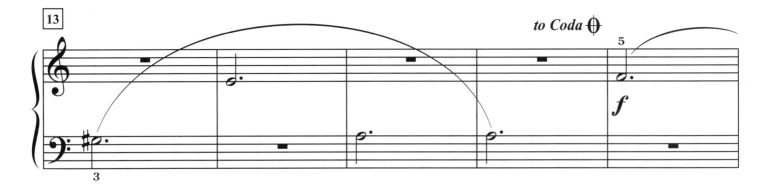

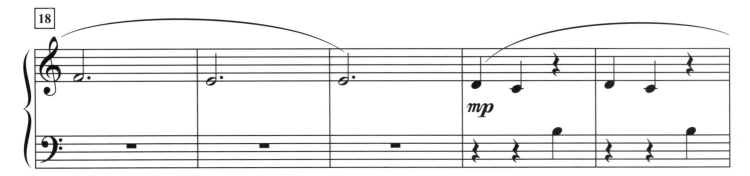

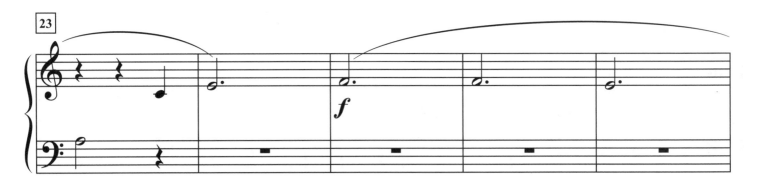

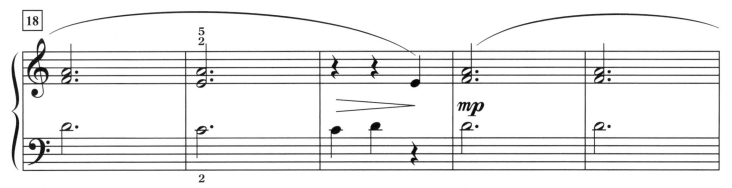

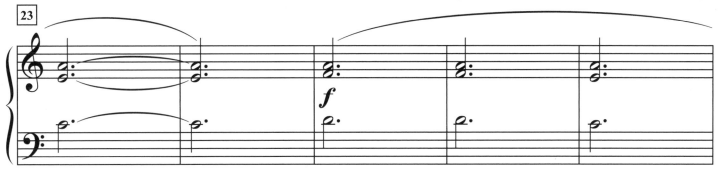

High

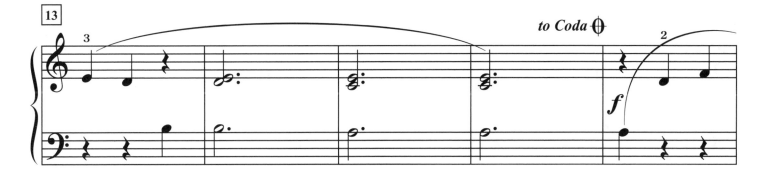

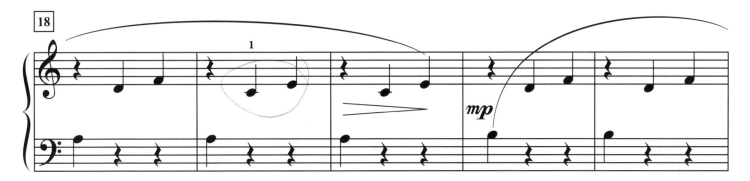

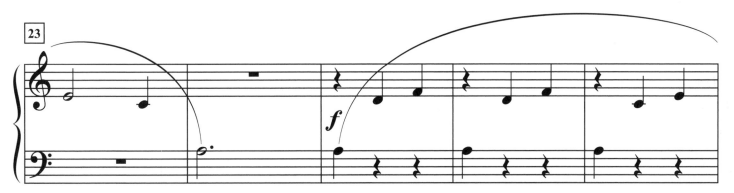

Middle

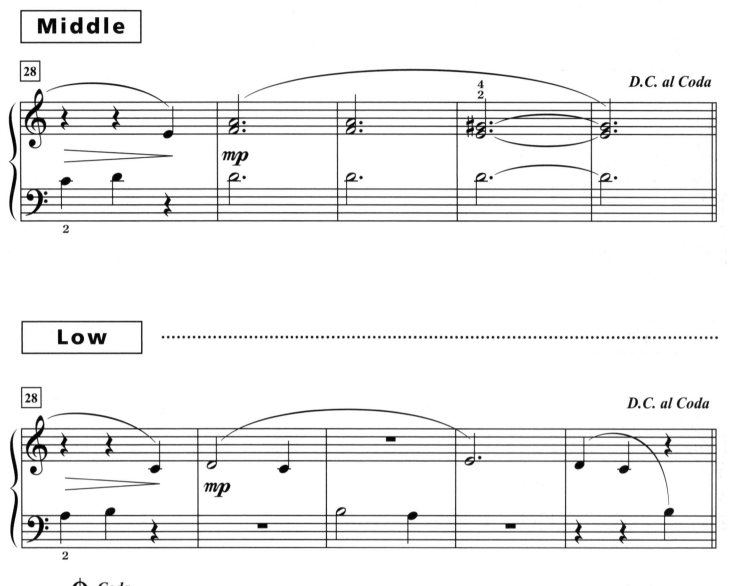

Low ·

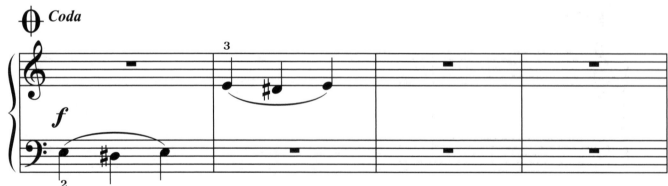

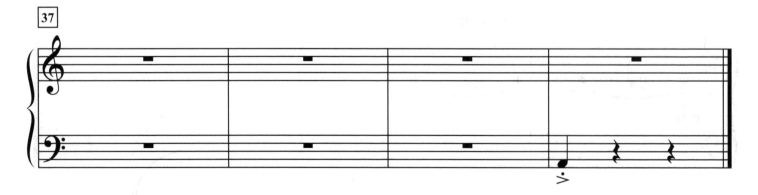

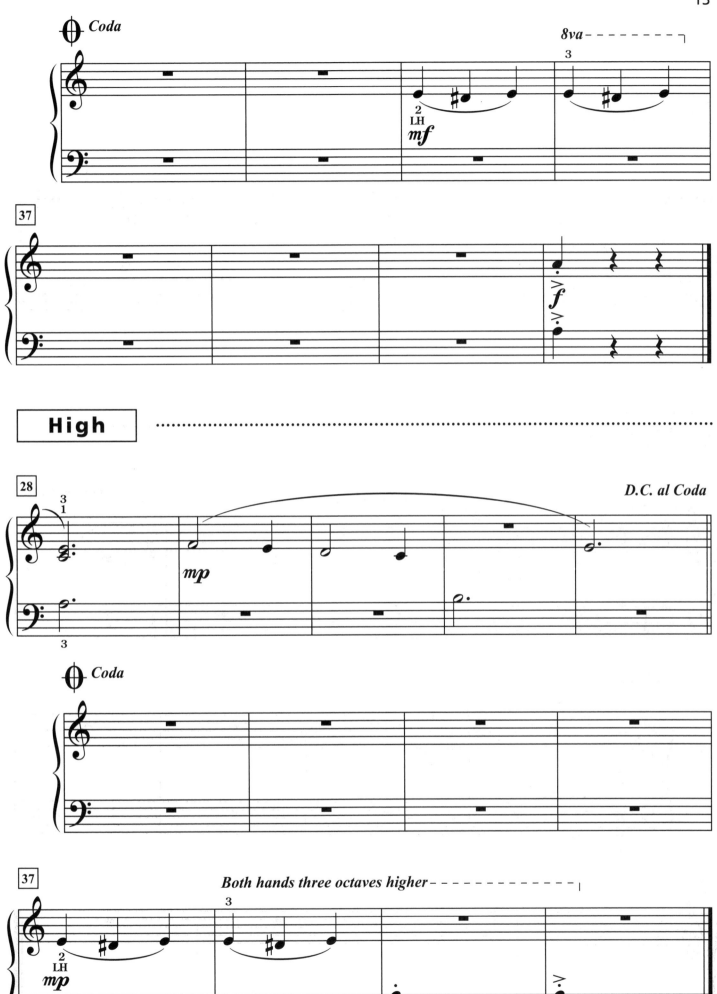

Sailing Open Waters

Melody Bober

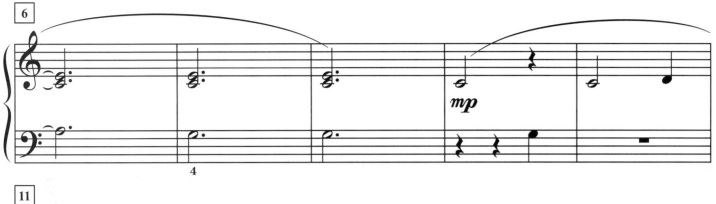

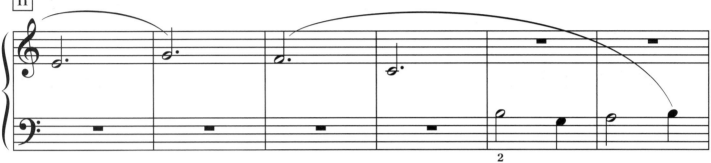

High

Lively (♩. = 80)

Both hands two octaves higher throughout

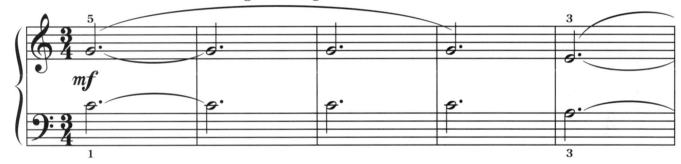

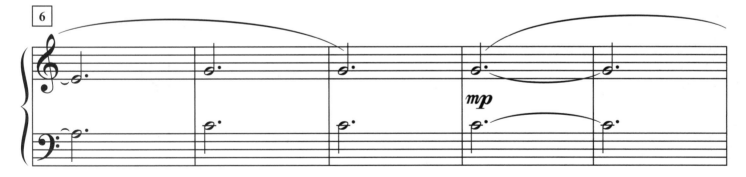

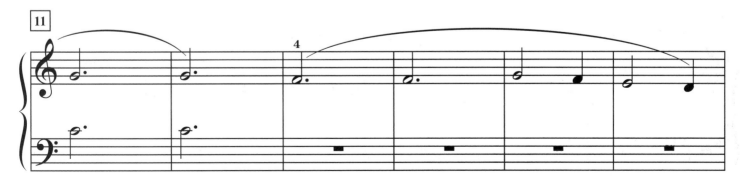

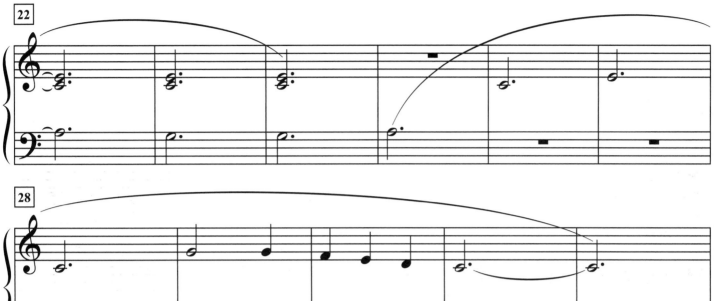

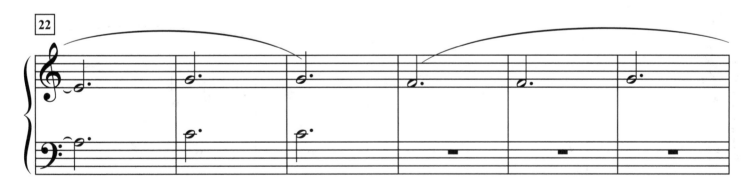

High

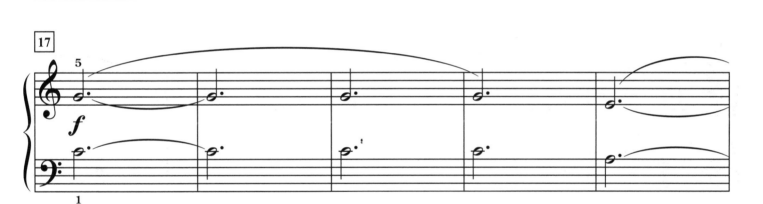

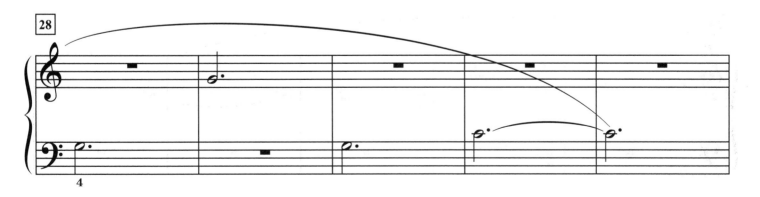

Middle

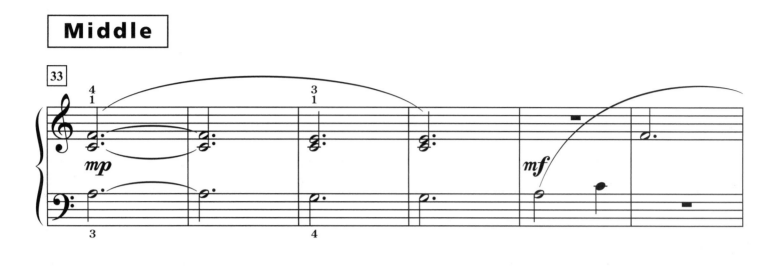

Low

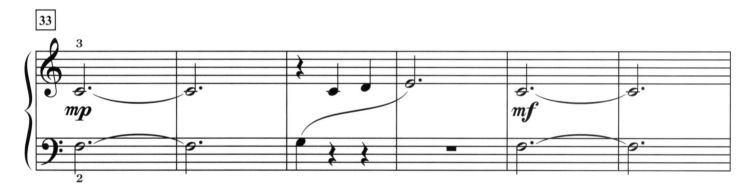

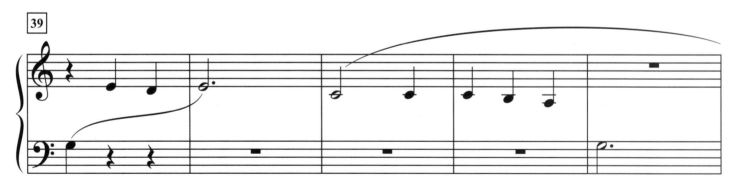

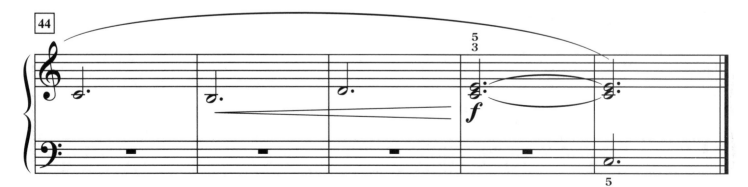

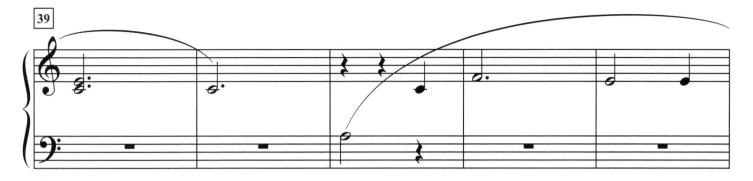

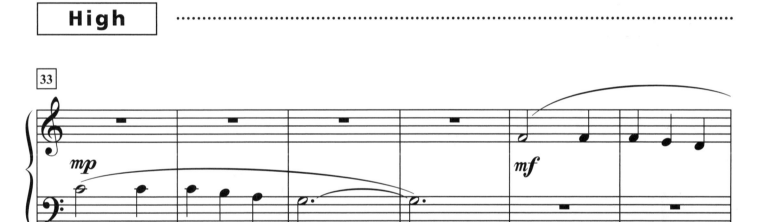

High ....

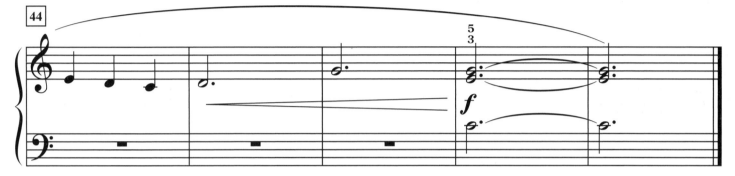

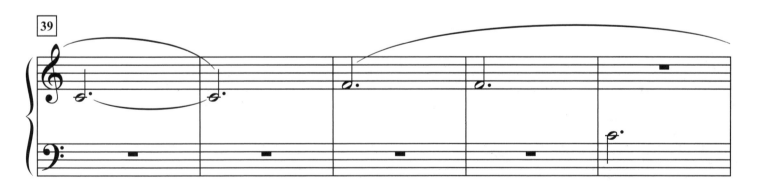

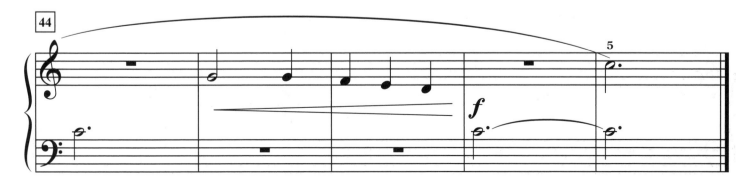

Three O'clock Chimes

Melody Bober

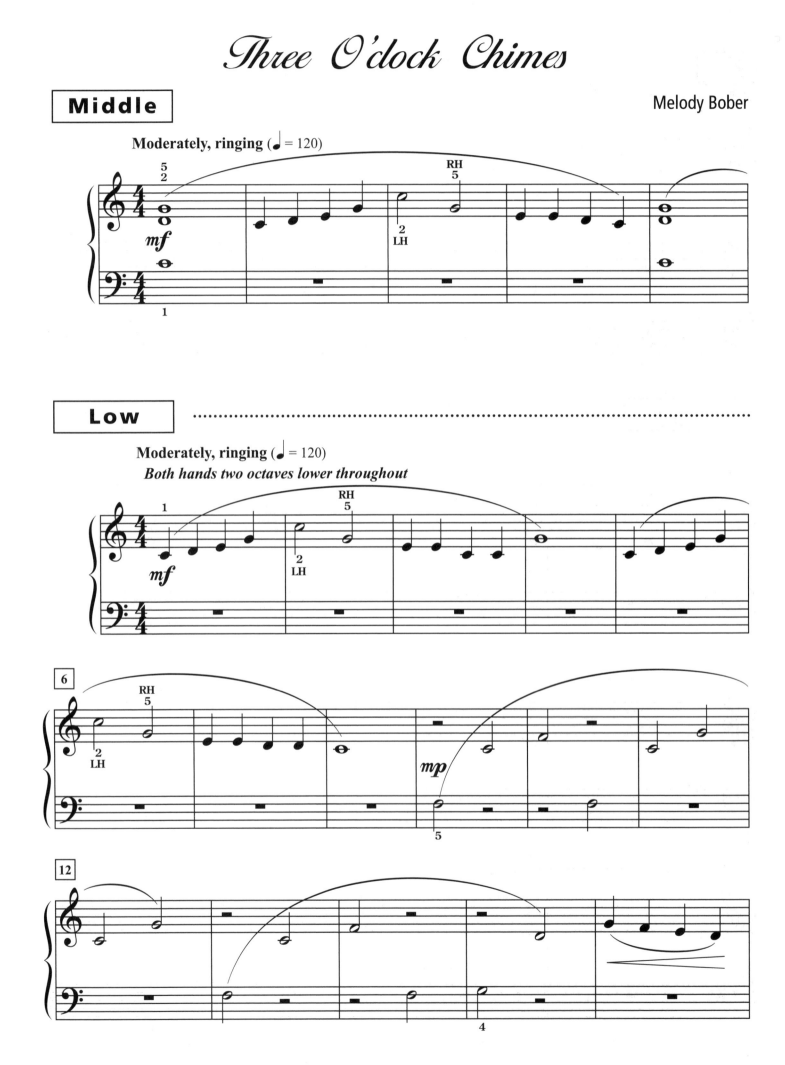

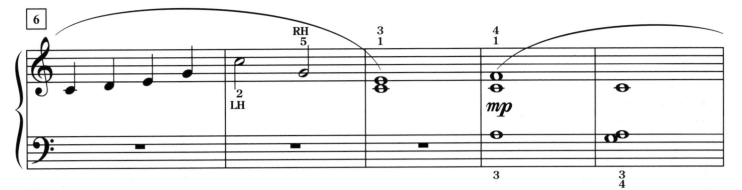

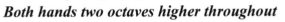

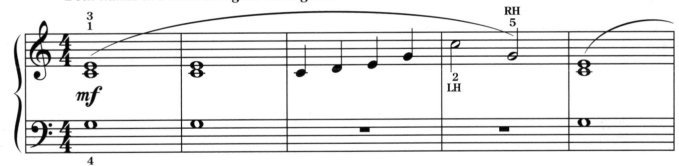

High

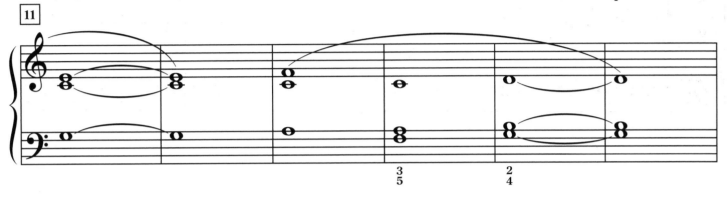

Moderately, ringing (♩ = 120)

Both hands two octaves higher throughout

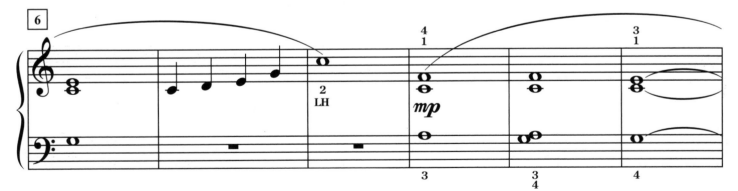

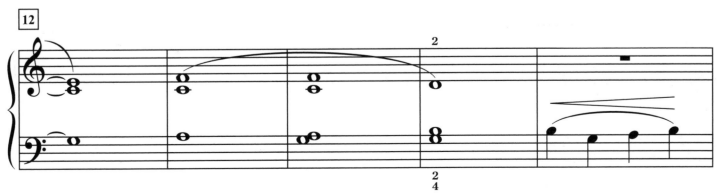

Middle

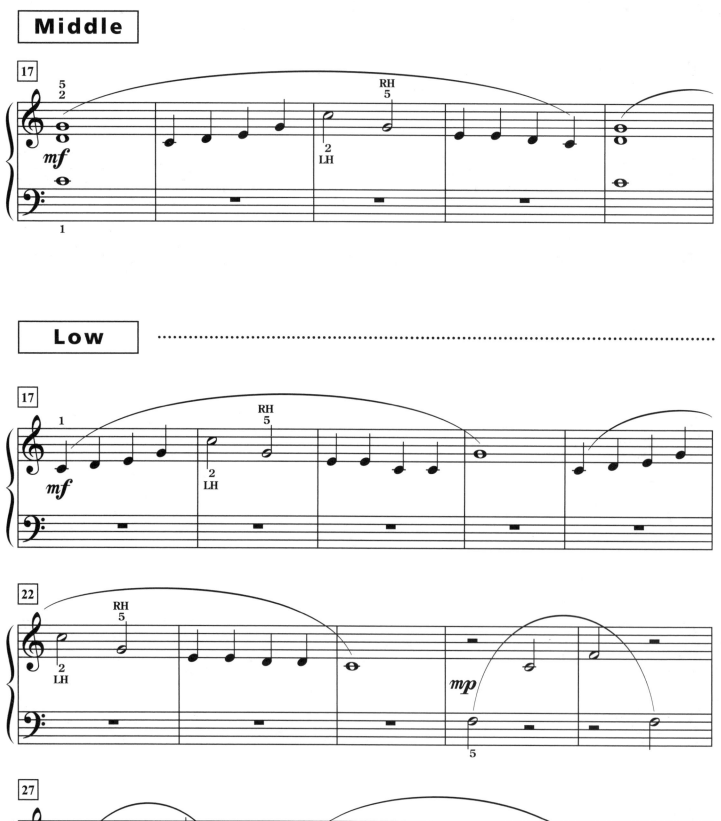

Low

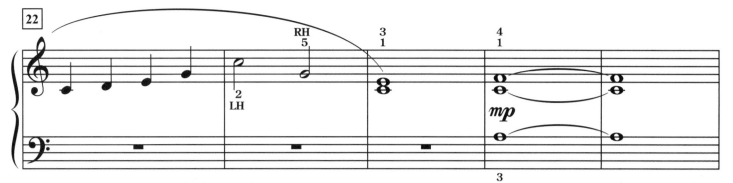

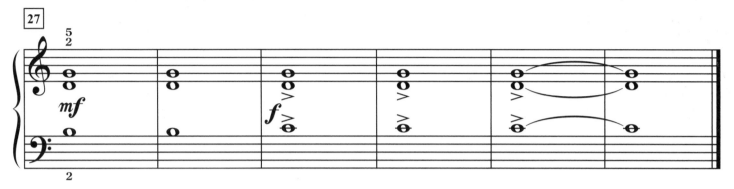

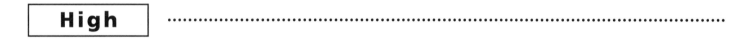

High . . . .

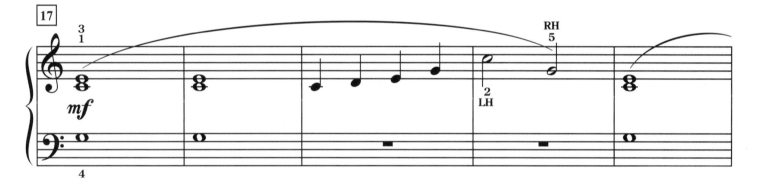

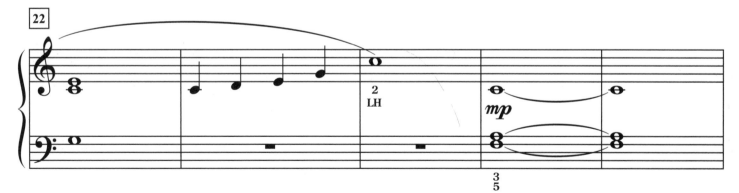

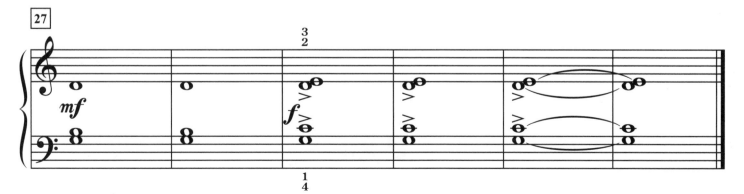